Wizard's World
Dot-to-Dot

Connect the Dots & Color

Evan & Lael Kimble

Illustrated by
Richard Salvucci

Sterling Publishing Co., Inc.
New York

By Evan and Lael Kimble
Illustrated by Richard Salvucci

10 9 8 7 6 5 4 3 2 1

Published by Sterling Publishing Co., Inc.
387 Park Avenue South, New York, NY 10016
© 2004 by Evan and Lael Kimble
Distributed in Canada by Sterling Publishing
^{c}/o Canadian Manda Group, One Atlantic Avenue, Suite 105
Toronto, Ontario, Canada M6K 3E7
Distributed in Great Britain and Europe by Chris Lloyd at Orca Book
Services, Stanley House, Fleets Lane, Poole BH15 3AJ, England
Distributed in Australia by Capricorn Link (Australia) Pty. Ltd.
P.O. Box 704, Windsor, NSW 2756, Australia

Sterling ISBN 1-4027-0995-1

CONTENTS

ALCHEMY

WHAT IS IT?
A method used by many wizards for changing matter.

WHERE AND WHEN:
The art of alchemy was handed down from the first century in Egypt and Arabia to Greece and Rome, and finally to western and central Europe.

ABILITIES:
Wizards believed that alchemy could turn metal into gold. They also thought it could give health and immortality.

DID YOU KNOW?
Gold was considered one of the most precious metals used in magic. Wizards put gold and silver in their wands to make them more powerful and to bring wealth, respect, and honor.

STORY:
The idea behind alchemy was that the wizard could take a substance and reduce it to its most basic state, and then transform it into its purest form. Some wizards would do this work on themselves, trying to make themselves better people.

The planets were connected with different metals and so were involved in the process of alchemy.

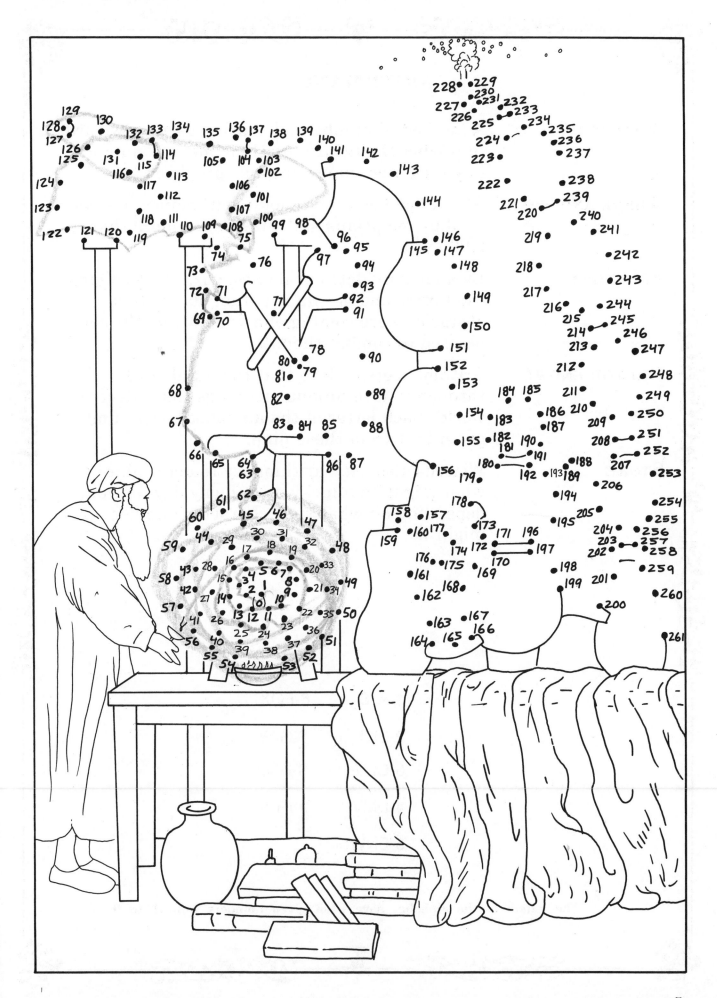

5

ARITHMANCY

WHAT IS IT? A method of number calculation used by wizards to predict the future. Arithmo means "number" in Greek, and mancy means "prophecy."

WHERE AND WHEN: Also known as numerology, arithmancy has been used by magicians and wizards for more than 2,000 years.

ABILITIES: By analyzing dates or names, wizards predicted the future and got information about what obstacles were coming and what strengths could be used to combat them.

DID YOU KNOW? Arithmancers believe that the numbers 1 through 9 have unique meanings that affect the world. Each letter of the alphabet has a number given to it from these nine.

STORY: Wizards also used arithmancy to determine what might be a lucky or unlucky day for you, depending on what your character number might be.

1-AJS	6-FOX
2-BKT	7-GPY
3-CLU	8-HQZ
4-DMV	9-IR
5-ENW	

The letters of the alphabet have been given numbers from 1 to 9.

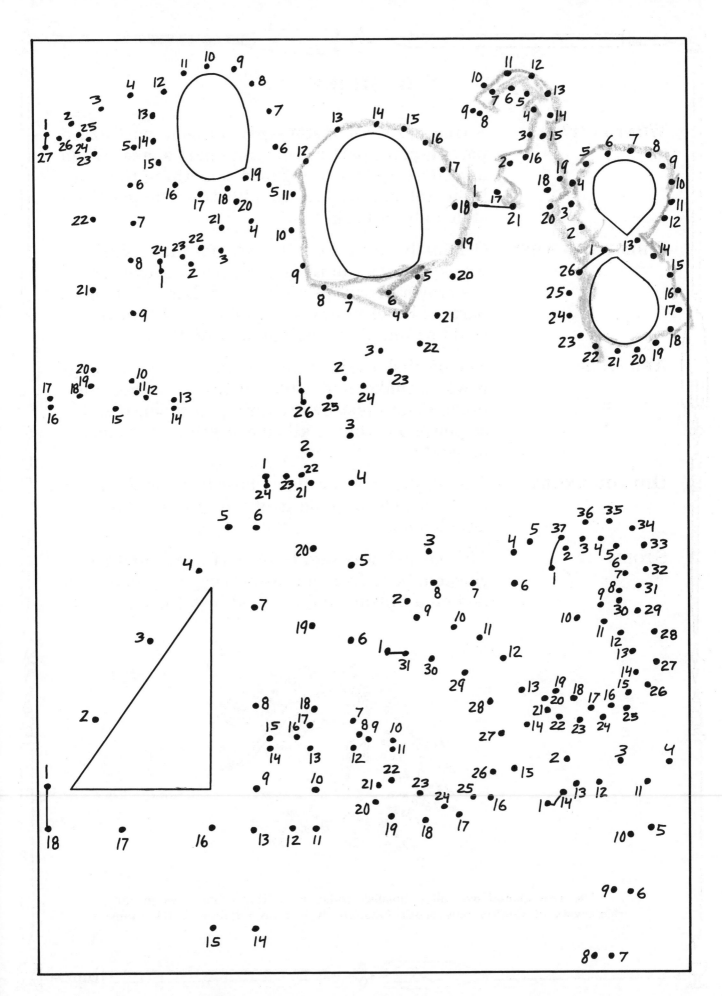

BASILISK

WHAT IS IT? A treacherous monster—part dragon, part lizard, part serpent, part rooster, and part snake. When a basilisk was used to guard something that had been stolen, a wizard would battle it to get the stolen object back.

WHERE AND WHEN: Originally, in first century Rome, the basilisk was known as the King of Serpents because of the crown markings on its head. Later, it took on parts of other animals. Legend had it that it could be found in England and Africa.

ABILITIES: The basilisk could stand on two feet even though it was a snake, and could set fire to bushes and break stones just by breathing on them. It was so poisonous that it killed everything it touched or saw.

DID YOU KNOW? The basilisk was probably based on the Egyptian cobra, which can hold itself upright and has a lethal venom.

STORY: The basilisk was said to be part snake and part chicken, born from a rooster's egg that had been laid on a hillside and hatched by a toad.

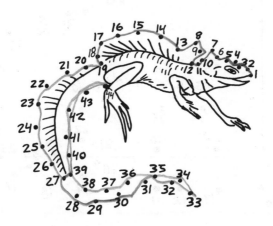

The real animal we call a basilisk today is a lizard that lives in the rainforests of Central and South America. It has no relation to the monster.

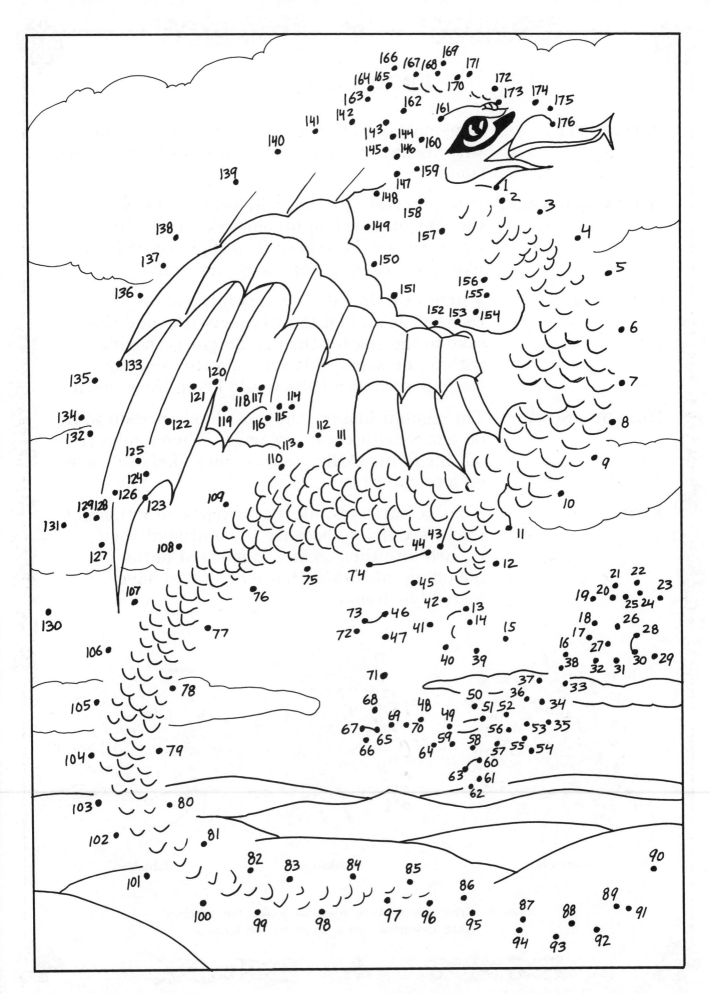

9

BROOMSTICK

WHAT IS IT? A magical object usually used by witches, but wizards have been known to use them in modern times.

WHERE AND WHEN: It is only recently that witches have been thought to travel on broomsticks. In earlier times, they were said to take flight on animals like goats, oxen, sheep, dogs, and wolves.

ABILITIES: Witches would rub a flying ointment on themselves and on their broomsticks and then take to the sky for their midnight gatherings with other witches. It was said that only the ringing of church bells would bring them down.

DID YOU KNOW? Throughout history, the most likely person to fly on a broomstick was a woman. When a man tried out his flying skills, he was more likely to travel on a pitchfork.

STORY: Some scientists think that witches only thought they were flying, because the ointment they rubbed into their skin was made of herbs including mandrake that made them have incredible dreams.

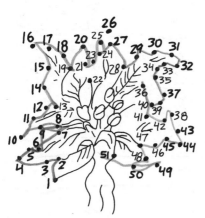

mandrake

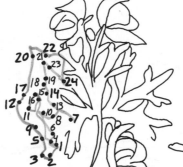

monkshood

nightshade

These herbs, which were used to make the witches' flying ointment, grew in most gardens.

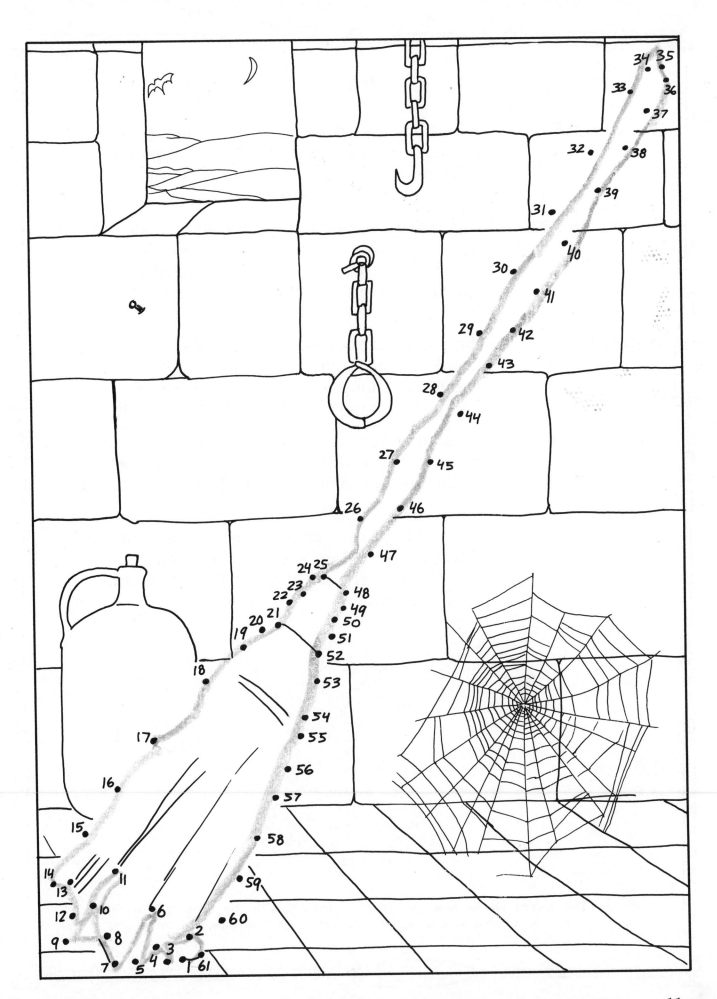

11

CAT

WHAT IS IT?

In the wizard's world, cats were thought to be magical creatures with supernatural powers. Sometimes wizards would change themselves into cats in order to go places without being seen.

WHERE AND WHEN:

Cats have been pets to people since 2000 B.C in Egypt. Witches, who often owned them, were said to make them into magical assistants called familiars, which could carry out their instructions.

ABILITIES:

Supposedly, cats could work spells and hypnotize people. A cat might be a witch in disguise. A witch was thought to be able to turn into a cat only nine times, once for each of a cat's lives.

DID YOU KNOW?

In ancient Greece, killing a cat was punishable by death, and when a family cat died, everyone in the house shaved their eyebrows in mourning.

STORY:

Some say cats are good luck, and some say that black cats, if they cross your path, are bad luck. There are also stories of witches riding black cats through the air at night in search of herbs for magic potions.

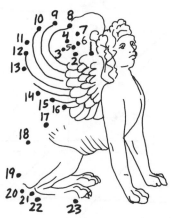

The sphinx was a magical creature, usually with the face of a woman, the body of a lion (a large wild cat), and the wings of an eagle.

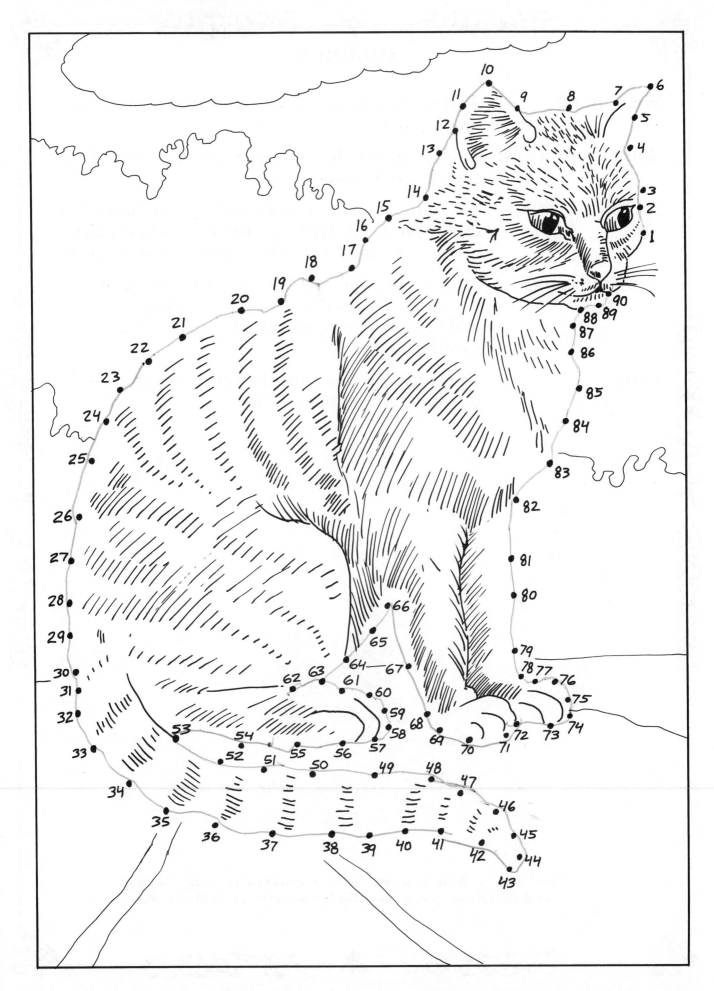

CAULDRON

WHAT IS IT?   A wizard's magical object, it is basically a huge cooking pot.

WHERE AND WHEN: The use of cauldrons dates back at least as far as ancient Greece and Rome.

ABILITIES: A wizard's most magical potions were concocted in the cauldron. With it a wizard could predict the future, and from it he could bestow wisdom.

DID YOU KNOW?   At one time, the cauldron was the center of the house. It was used not only for cooking and making medicines, but also for bathing and washing clothes.

STORY: The cauldron was once thought to be the gateway to the underworld.

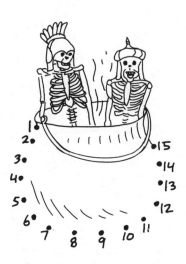

There was an Irish king who used a cauldron to bring "undead" soldiers (ghosts) back from the underworld to fight for him.

15

CENTAUR

WHAT IS IT?   An immortal creature that is half man and half horse. Wizards and centaurs often got together to discuss matters of the forest.

WHERE AND WHEN: There was a legend that herds of centaurs lived in the mountains of northern Greece.

ABILITIES: With the head and torso of a man but the body and hind quarters of a horse, centaurs were often beautiful and good, but always rowdy, wild, and ready to fight.

DID YOU KNOW?   Some centaurs didn't have wild ways and were wise, just, and scholarly. One such creature was called Chiron, and he trained the great Greek heroes Achilles and Hercules.

STORY: Chiron chose to give up his immortality when he was accidentally wounded by a poisoned arrow belonging to Hercules. When the pain became too great, he asked the king of the Gods, Zeus, to allow him to die. Zeus did, but immortalized him in the sky in the constellation Centaurus.

Like the centaur, the satyr was part human—the top half was like a man, but the lower half was all goat.

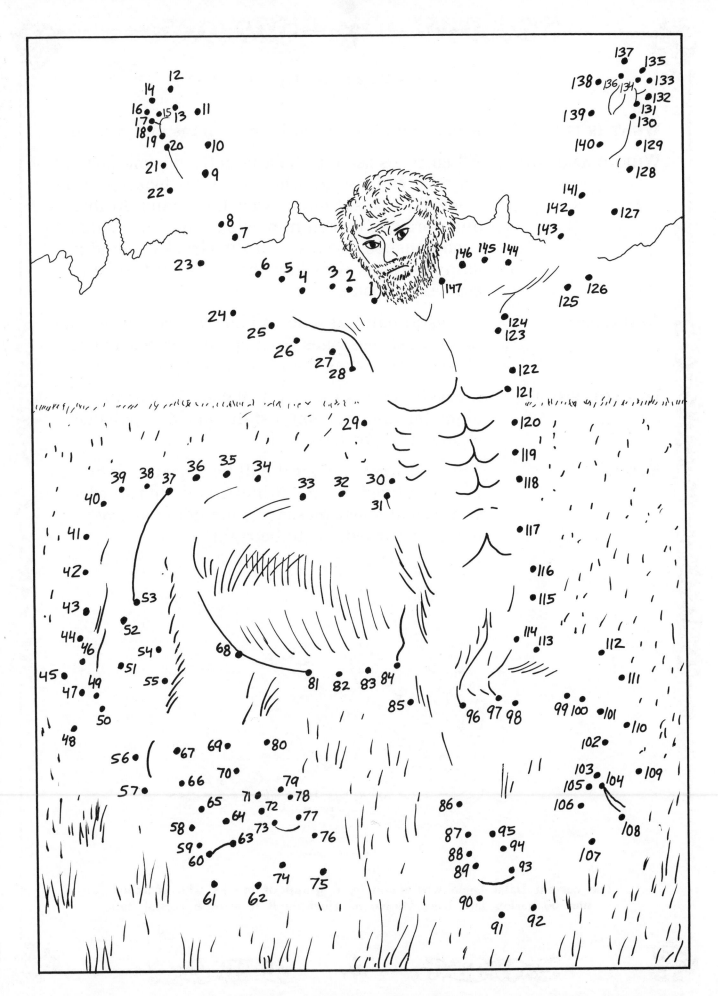

17

CRYSTAL BALL

WHAT IS IT?   A magical object used by magicians and wizards.

WHERE AND WHEN: All cultures seem to have practiced some form of scrying, which is another name for looking into something to see an answer. Egyptians, Arabs, and Persians looked in bowls of ink, the Romans used polished crystal, and the Greeks peered into shiny mirrors. Kids have been thought to be especially good scryers.

ABILITIES: A crystal ball was said to help wizards to see the future, get messages from spirits, or get a vision of something they might need to know.

DID YOU KNOW?   A crystal ball is usually 4 inches (10 cm) in diameter and rests on a stand made of polished ebony, ivory, or boxwood.

STORY: The best known crystal ball belonged to John Dee who lived in the 16th century. He recorded volumes of spirit messages, including at least one that turned out to be right!

The current Dalai Lama was found by a group of monks who searched for him by gazing into Lake Lhotso in Tibet as if it were a crystal ball.

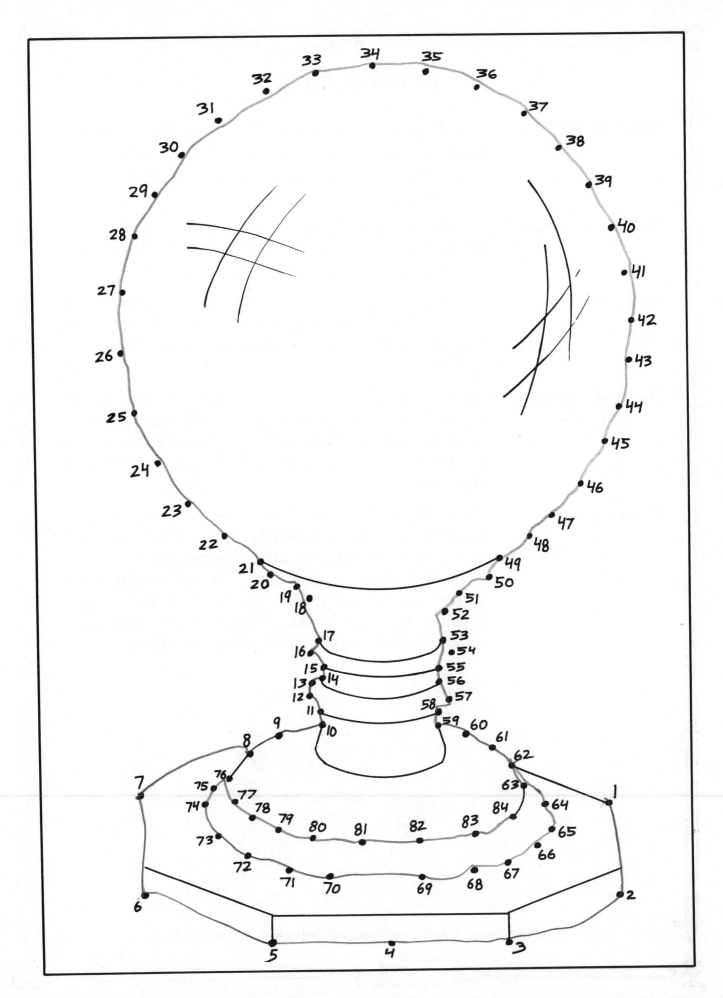

19

CRYSTAL CAVE

WHAT IS IT?
The Crystal Cave was a place that Merlin the wizard went to as a young man. Fire light reflected from the crystal walls created visions of the future.

WHERE AND WHEN:
Merlin grew up in what is now Wales in Great Britain, and stories about him date at least as far back as the twelfth century.

ABILITIES:
In the cave, Merlin learned how to interpret his visions, how to make potions and medicines, and how to understand the language of the beasts and birds.

DID YOU KNOW?
As a child, Merlin was feared and disliked by his family and countrymen because he was quiet, strange, and had odd powers. These powers were nurtured by Galapas, an old wizard who lived in the Cave.

STORY:
After Merlin had been away, he returned to the Crystal Cave to seek out Galapas. Near the cave in a patch of grass, Galapas' bones were scattered about in the dirt. Merlin laid the bones to rest and began to occupy the cave, just like Galapas used to do. Eventually Merlin not only looked like Galapas, but had his wisdom.

Merlin never found out what had happened to his old teacher.

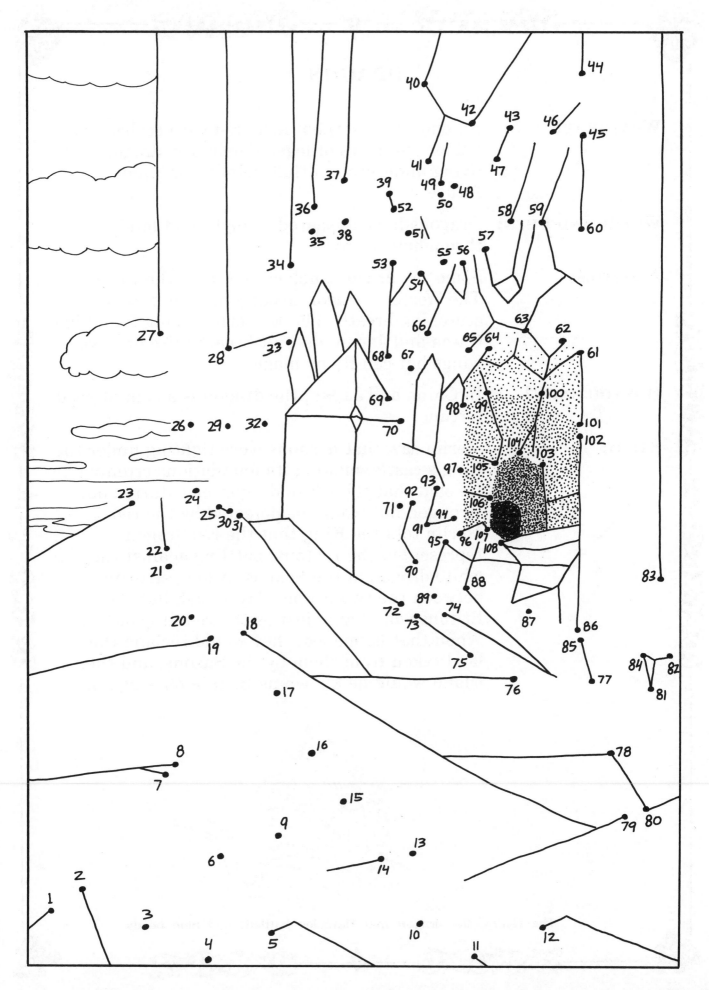

DRAGON

WHAT IS IT?   An enormous serpent armored with scales and one or two pairs of legs. Merlin saw dragons living underground that helped him predict the future.

WHERE AND WHEN: Dragons have appeared in myth and folklore throughout history.

ABILITIES: Some say dragons helped to create the world. The Western dragon usually has wings and a scorching breath. The Eastern dragon, found in China and Japan, doesn't breathe fire or have wings but can fly by magic.

DID YOU KNOW?   In China and Japan, the dragon is a sign of good fortune.

STORY: Merlin saw that dragons were fighting under the King's castle, making its foundations crumble. He said that the white dragon had started out stronger, but would be defeated by the red. Merlin told the King that the red dragon represented the Britons, battling against the white dragon of the Saxons. A long struggle between the two peoples lay ahead, but the Britons would win, just as the red dragon had. When that happened, they would reclaim the land taken from them by the Saxons, and their island would be known as Britain once again.

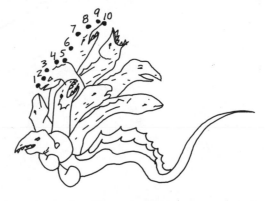

The Hydra, the dragon that Hercules battled, had nine heads.

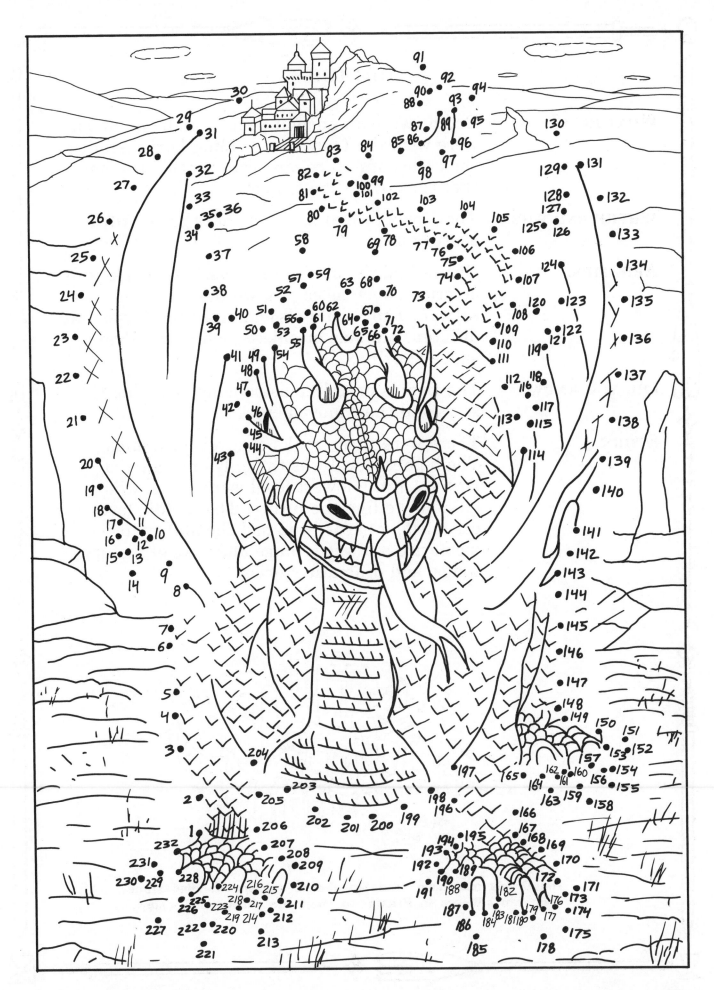

23

DRUIDS

WHAT IS IT? Druids were an ancient people, many of whom were wizards. They used healing herbs, studied the cycles of nature, and could recognize omens that came from the animals.

WHERE AND WHEN: They lived in Britain as far back as the fifth century B.C.

ABILITIES: Druids had the ability to transform people into creatures such as eagles, wolfhounds, and salmon. They could also change themselves into different animals or objects, which is called shape-shifting.

DID YOU KNOW? The Druids practiced astronomy, studying the stars and their movements.

STORY: There were three ranks or levels of Druids. The highest level was the only one called a Druid. On the lowest level were vates, who were gifted at telling the future. The middle level was occupied by bards, who had the ability to memorize and recite huge amounts of history, songs, and dramatic stories.

The Druids may have used Stonehenge, ancient standing stones you can still see in Britain, to chart the change of seasons.

DWARF

WHAT IS IT?   In the wizard's world, dwarves were small magical beings, usually men, who had long gray beards. Wizards sometimes called on dwarves to go on adventures. If gold was involved, dwarves were always game to go.

WHERE AND WHEN: Dwarves have appeared for a long time in the folklore of Germany, Scandinavia, and Great Britain.

ABILITIES: In legends, dwarves guarded magnificent treasures buried deep underground. They were gifted metalworkers and made beautiful and sometimes magical objects, including weapons. They could become invisible or assume any shape, and could also see the future.

DID YOU KNOW?   Some said they were immortal, or they may have lived for hundreds of years.

STORY: Dwarves made a magical spear for the Norse God Odin that always hit its target.

Some say that dwarves had the feet of a goose, a crow, or a goat.

ELEMENTALS

WHAT IS IT? An elemental is a spirit of air, fire, water, or earth. Wizards worked with elementals to get information or to make things happen.

WHERE AND WHEN: People have believed in elementals for thousands of years.

ABILITIES: Any magical work would have to begin with calling on the elementals. With them, a wizard could bring about rain, fertility, wealth, love, and many other things.

DID YOU KNOW? Wizards called upon the earth to help bring about riches, the air to bring intelligence or intuition, fire to give extra power to a spell, and water to help with any spell that had to do with feelings.

STORY: Every wizard and many ancient civilizations believed that the elements called earth, air, fire, and water made up everything in the world. It was often thought that all knowledge was encoded in these elements, and that this knowledge was also in us since we are made up of these elements too.

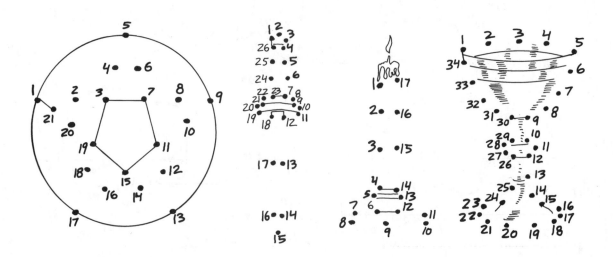

Each elemental has a particular magical tool that goes with it.

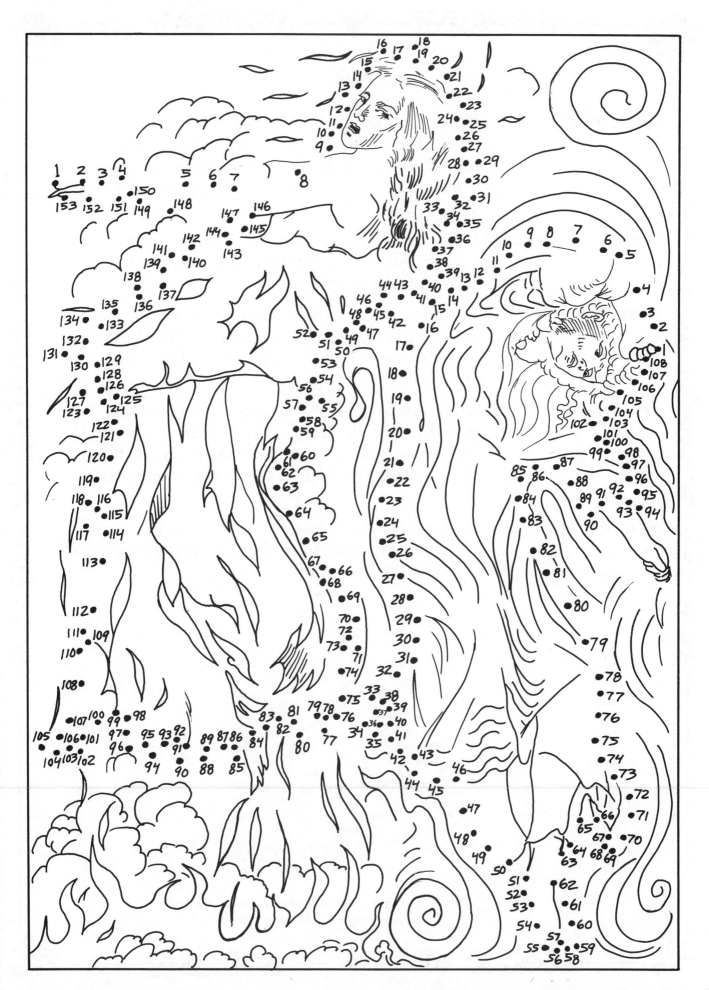

ELF

WHAT IS IT? In English folklore, male elves were wizened old men, while female elves were lovely golden-haired maidens. Elves and wizards often had common interests, and sometimes battled side by side to fight evil.

WHERE AND WHEN: Elves have appeared in the folklore of many nations for a very long time, especially in the Northern Hemisphere.

ABILITIES: Elves use their supernatural powers to meddle in human life. Most are said to resemble humans, but they can change shape or vanish in the blink of an eye.

DID YOU KNOW? Some kinds of elves are called house elves. They will actually do chores and help in a household. But if you give a house elf a piece of clothing, that means he's free to leave and stop working for you.

STORY: In the folklore of Iceland and Germany, elves stole babies, cattle, and food and caused disease in people and animals.

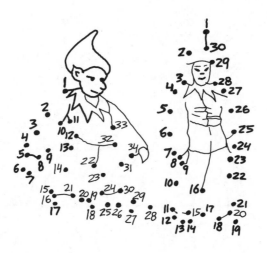

There are many stories about Santa Claus having helpers who are elves.

31

FAIRY

WHAT IS IT? The fairy is an immortal, supernatural being who is only occasionally seen by people. It could be large or small, nice or mean, scary or funny, beautiful or ugly. Fairies and wizards are among the oldest creatures in the world.

WHERE AND WHEN: All over the world and in all times, there have been stories about fairies.

ABILITIES: Usually fairies are kind to human beings, but when they think they have been crossed, they can be very tricky and cruel. They often steal mortal children and replace them with fairy babies—changelings. And if they give a gift—turning something into gold or a pumpkin into a carriage—the gift is likely to change back again.

DID YOU KNOW? The word fairy comes from the Latin "fata" meaning "goddess of fate"; like the Fates, fairies were thought to control people's lives.

STORY: The Tooth Fairy is talked about in English-speaking countries and in Spain. Completely trustworthy, she is said to visit in the night to leave money or small gifts in return for baby teeth left under a child's pillow.

Before the Tooth Fairy, there used to be stories of a Tooth Mouse, and kids would place teeth by mouse holes in exchange for candy or coins.

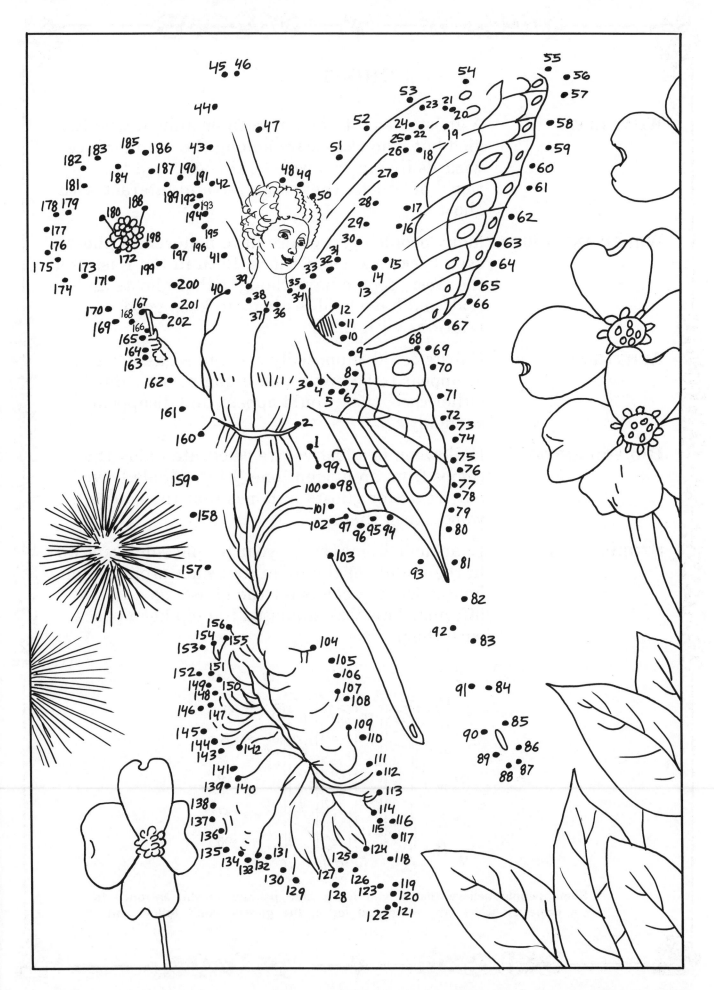

GHOST

WHAT IS IT?   A ghost is said to be a person or animal who has died but who reappears among the living. Since wizards live in two worlds, this one and the world of spirits, they often see and interact with ghosts.

WHERE AND WHEN: Many people everywhere have believed in ghosts, even back to ancient times. Both in the East and the West, people have thought that ghosts are real, and have held festivals to keep good relations with them.

ABILITIES: Ghosts could supposedly come in a gassy vapor or appear to be just like a living person. But in either case, they would appear and disappear suddenly.

DID YOU KNOW?   Halloween is a festival we celebrate today that comes from an ancient one. In it, people leave out treats for ghosts in hopes that the spirits won't harm them.

STORY: In ancient Rome, every year people would get up in the middle of the night and walk around their houses leaving beans for the ghosts as an offering. This was supposed to help keep peace with them.

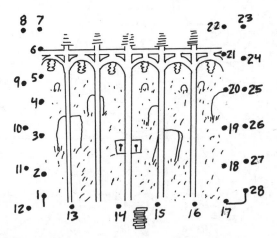

Some people believe that if you leave nine pennies at the entrance to a cemetery when you enter and leave, the ghosts won't follow you.

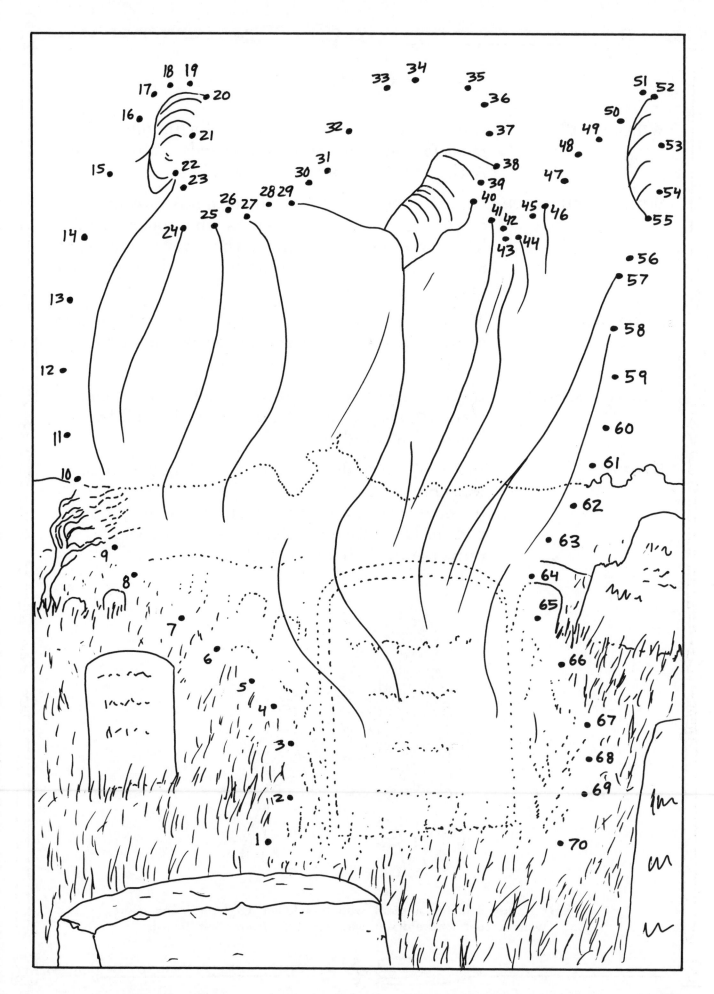

GIANT

WHAT IS IT?   Any really immense creature. Merlin, one of the most famous and powerful wizards, helped King Arthur to defeat a terrible giant.

WHERE AND WHEN: Giants appear in the myths of many cultures, often as a race of huge beings who appeared even before the gods. Sometimes they were thought of as worthy enemies, and knights would seek to do battle with them.

ABILITIES: The earliest giants were as tall as mountains and amazingly strong. Later ones were cruel and would steal women and children.

DID YOU KNOW?   In "Jack and the Beanstalk," Jack hides from a giant who says, "Fee, Fi, Fo, Fum, I smell the blood of an Englishman!"

STORY: In Greek mythology, the Giants, called Titans, were born from the union of earth and sky, and in some cases had three heads. They fought the gods of Olympus and almost destroyed the universe in their fierce battles.

King Arthur defeated a giant who had killed 15 kings. The giant wore a coat embroidered with the hair from their beards.

GRIFFIN

WHAT IS IT?   The griffin was thought to be a monster with the body of a lion, the head and wings of an eagle, and a back covered with feathers.

WHERE AND WHEN: The first stories of griffins appeared in Egypt and the Middle East in 3300 B.C. India was thought to be the native country of the griffins.

ABILITIES: They would attack any living thing and carry it in their huge claws to their nests in the mountains.

DID YOU KNOW?   Griffins, like dragons, were symbols of wisdom.

STORY: Griffins found gold in the mountains and built their nests of it. Since hunters came looking for the gold, the griffins were forced to keep vigilant guard over their nests. They did their best to keep plunderers at a distance.

The griffin was used in art as an emblem of courage.

HAG

WHAT IS IT? A supernatural being that takes the form of an old woman.

WHERE AND WHEN: Stories of hags come from the British Isles and are ancient.

ABILITIES: Hags can be nice or vicious. One that is an ancient nature spirit is responsible for changes in the weather. Others are like witches and torment and sometimes eat people.

DID YOU KNOW? The most famous English hag was Black Annis. She had blue skin, long teeth, and claws of iron.

STORY: The storm hag, from Scotland, was an ancient goddess known as Cailleach Bheare. She had a blue face and only one eye, white hair, and looked like the gnarled branches of a tree. She is said to have created the islands off the coast of Scotland.

The storm hag uses her magic wand to cover the crops with frost after Halloween.

LADY OF THE LAKE

WHAT IS IT?   The Lady of the Lake, also called Vivien or Nimue, was the high priestess of a pagan religion that existed at the time of Merlin.

WHERE AND WHEN: The Merlin legends date at least as far back as the twelfth century. The Lady of the Lake was said to live in a place called Avalon, a sacred island some think is now Glastonbury in England.

ABILITIES: The Lady of the Lake had fantastic powers and is said to have given King Arthur the great and magical sword, Excalibur.

DID YOU KNOW?   Ancient people have always believed in water goddesses, like the Lady of the Lake, and the practice of throwing money into wells and fountains may have come from this type of worship.

STORY: Merlin fell deeply in love with the Lady of the Lake and agreed to teach her all his skills. She became so powerful that her magic outshone even Merlin's. Determined not to be enslaved by him, she imprisoned the old man in a glass tower.

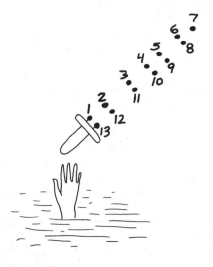

When Arthur was mortally wounded, he had one of his knights give the sword Excalibur back to the Lady of the Lake.

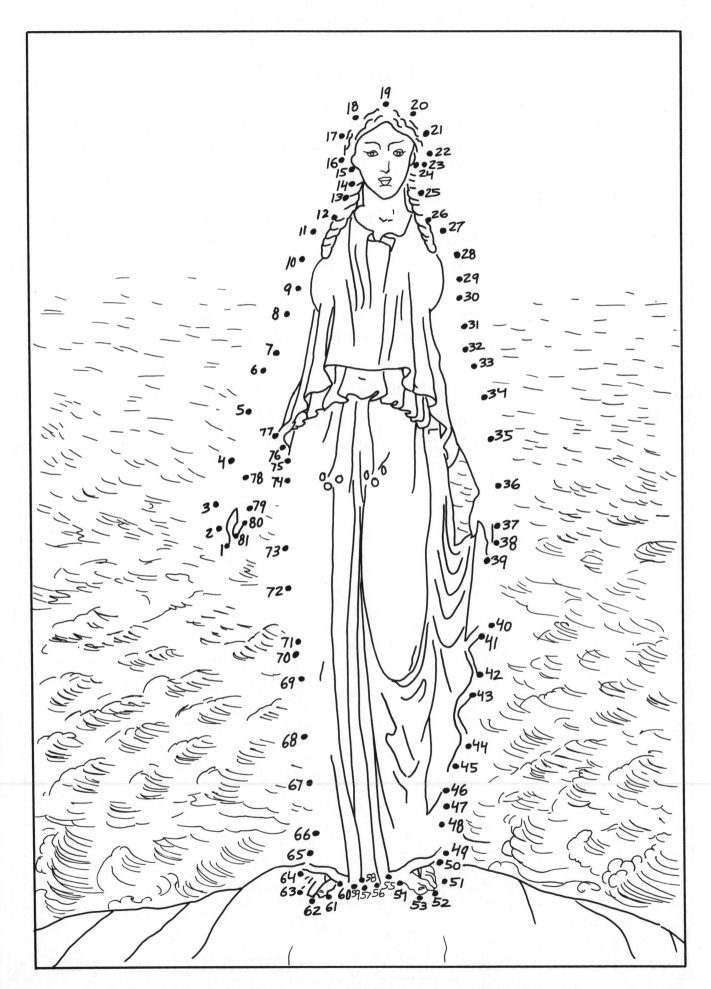

MAGIC WAND

WHAT IS IT? A stick about 14 or 15 inches (36 or 38 cm) long that wizards used for magical purposes. It was made of wood, clay, or metal.

WHERE AND WHEN: Magic wands first appeared in ancient cave paintings. They were used by the Egyptians, by Druids, Moses, the ancient Greeks, Merlin, and others to do amazing things.

ABILITIES: Magic wands were used to cast all kinds of spells, from raising someone from the dead to changing a pumpkin into a coach.

DID YOU KNOW? Some magic wands had special letters carved on the side of them and crystals attached.

STORY: The Greek god Hermes used his wand to make himself invisible to men.

Stage magicians today often use magic wands, like when they pull a rabbit out of a hat.

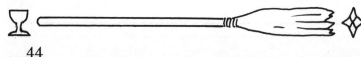

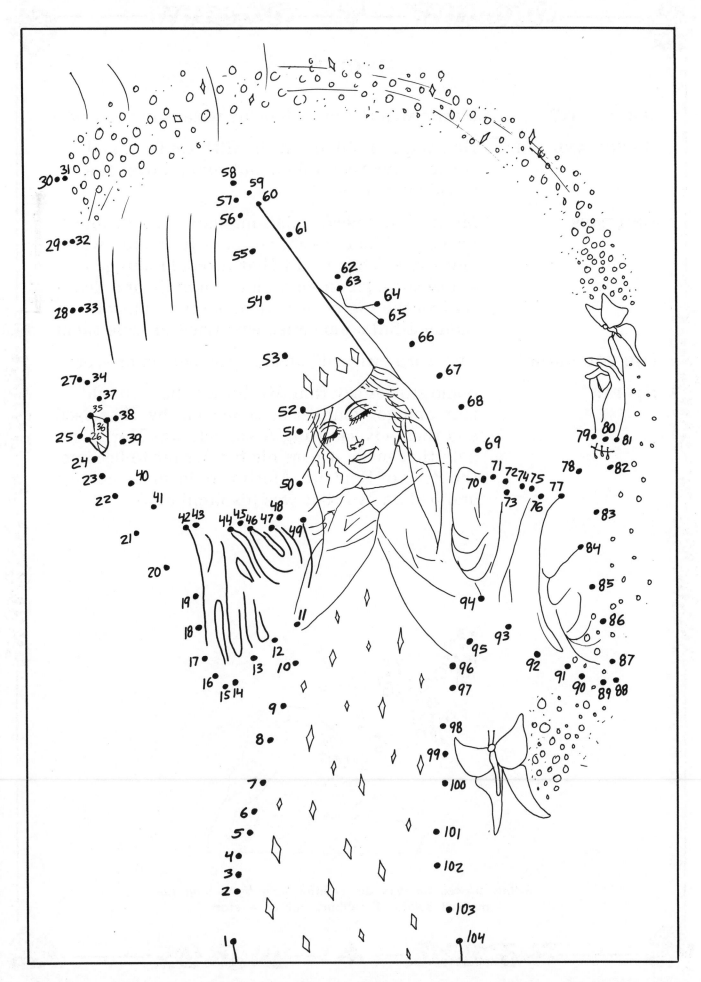

MERLIN

WHAT IS IT?   Merlin was the most famous wizard in the world.

WHERE AND WHEN: He lived in England in the fifth century, and stories have been told about him all over the world ever since.

ABILITIES: Merlin could perform all manner of spells and tricks, and had special powers over metal, water, and stone. This meant that he could plunge a sword through an anvil, make a millstone float, control the raging sea, or make the walls of Camelot fall on enemies who tried to scale them.

DID YOU KNOW?   The word "wizard" means wise person or seer.

STORY: Some stories say that Merlin was born an old man and got younger as time went by. He raised and then advised King Arthur. It was Merlin's help that made it possible for Arthur to become the King of England. Merlin could shape-change and had an owl that was his familiar.

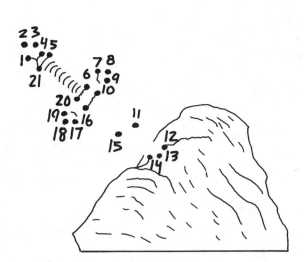

Arthur proved he was the rightful king by pulling the magical sword, Excalibur, out of a stone.

MORGANA LE FAY

WHAT IS IT?   Morgana Le Fay was a sorceress who lived in the time of Merlin.

WHERE AND WHEN: Since the thirteenth century, Morgana has been mentioned in the books and legends of Britain, Italy, and France.

ABILITIES: She was the sister or half-sister of King Arthur. Morgana could conjure, enchant, fly through the air, appear as an animal, and heal with magic herbs.

DID YOU KNOW?   "Le fay" means "the fairy" in French.

STORY: When Arthur was wounded in battle, Morgana brought him to Avalon, set him on a golden bed, and made him well. Some say she learned her magical skills from Merlin.

As time went on, Morgana was seen as an evil person, and it is said that she tried to destroy her brother.

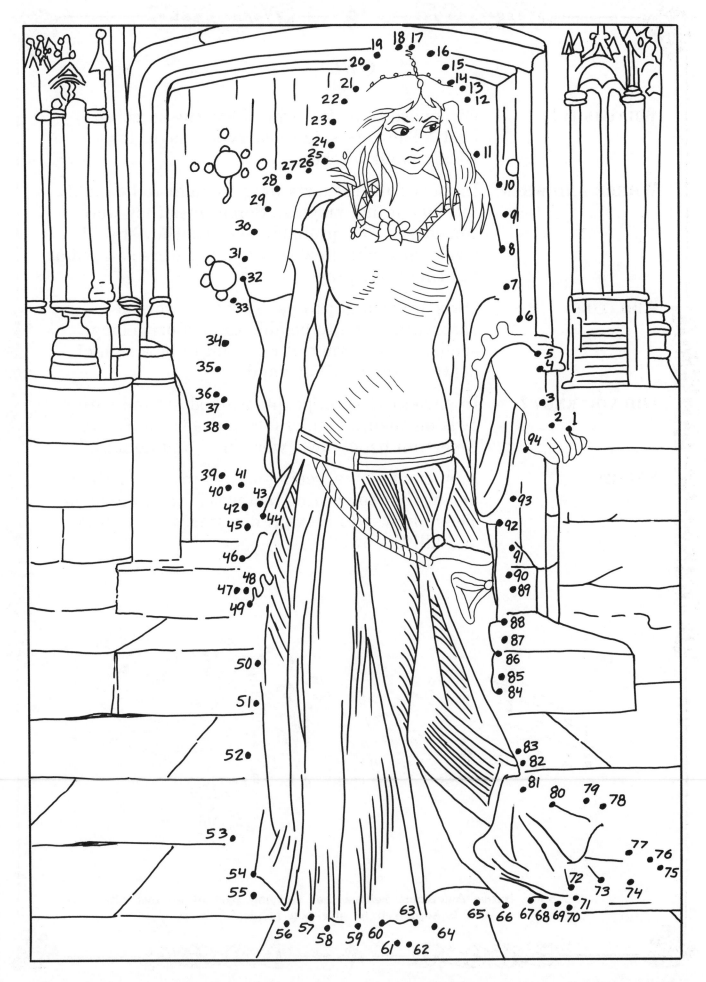

OWL

WHAT IS IT? Owls used to be thought of as "the sorcerer's bird." They are said to carry messages for wizards and witches.

WHERE AND WHEN: In most cultures owls were thought to be highly intelligent and magical. Sometimes they were considered evil, probably because they stayed awake at night, flew silently, and were so good at hunting their prey.

ABILITIES: Owls are thought to have great powers of observation and to be able to memorize long spells. Their eerie call was said to be a sign of death or some evil at hand.

DID YOU KNOW? In ancient Greece, people walked around with owls on their shoulders or in cages. In Native American belief, owls were kind and helpful.

STORY: In ancient Rome, seeing an owl in the daytime meant that something bad was going to happen. The only way to prevent disaster was to catch and kill the owl.

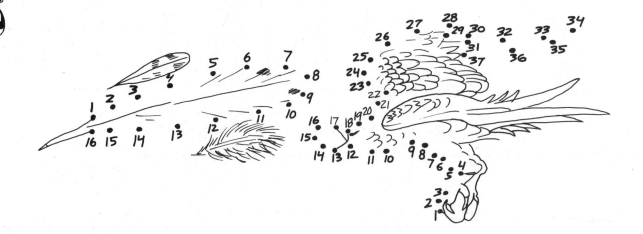

Some Native Americans believe that carrying part of an owl with you is supposed to give you magical powers.

PHOENIX

WHAT IS IT?   The phoenix is a mysterious fictional bird, a little larger than an eagle, magnificently colored in purple, gold, red, and blue. A wizard may keep a phoenix as a companion and to protect himself.

WHERE AND WHEN: Stories of the phoenix were common in ancient Egypt, Greece, and Rome. They also appeared in China, where the phoenix stood for power and integrity.

ABILITIES: Every five hundred years, this bird would set itself on fire, be reduced to ashes, and rise from the ashes to be reborn. Because of this it has become a symbol of immortality.

DID YOU KNOW?   Legend has it that there was only one phoenix in the world, and it lived in Arabia.

STORY: The phoenix ate frankincense, myrrh, and cinnamon, and when it came to the end of its life, it would build a nest out of these ingredients and then flap its wings so quickly that it burst into flames.

According to some stories, after rising from the ashes, the bird would gather them up and make them into an egg, which it brought to Egypt to the temple of the sun god. This act assured it of five more centuries of life.

53

POTION

WHAT IS IT?   A drink, brewed by a wizard, that has magical powers. The word potion comes from the Latin potio, meaning "drink."

WHERE AND WHEN: The use of potions goes back at least as far as ancient Greece and Rome.

ABILITIES: Old legends and fairy tales speak of sleep potions, love potions, potions of forgetfulness, and potions to cause jealousy and strife. Some potions were said to cause the body to change shape.

DID YOU KNOW?   A potion might call for bats' blood, crushed beetles, toads, feathers, or lizards, as well as herbs.

STORY: The use of toads in potions may have been for the substance that toads give off when frightened, sometimes called "toad's milk." It could cause hallucinations and speed up the heart rate.

As time went by, potions used fewer animal parts and more herbs.

SALAMANDER

WHAT IS IT?   Like the toad and the frog, the salamander is an amphibian, living both in and out of the water. It is a small lizard, and its skin has some qualities that briefly keep it from burning. That is how it got to be thought of as a nature spirit.

WHERE AND WHEN: The salamander was first seen as a magical creature in ancient Greece and Rome.

ABILITIES: The salamander was thought to be able to withstand fire. People had seen salamanders appear in the fire and got the idea that they were not only able to stay alive in fire, but even craved it.

DID YOU KNOW?   At one time, fireproof clothing was labeled "salamander wool."

STORY: The salamander represents the fire elemental, so wizards would use salamanders or call on them to help bring more power to a spell. Wizards also used salamanders in potions.

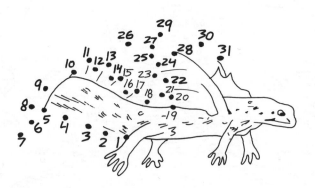

Some people claimed that salamanders had wings and could fly, like miniature dragons.

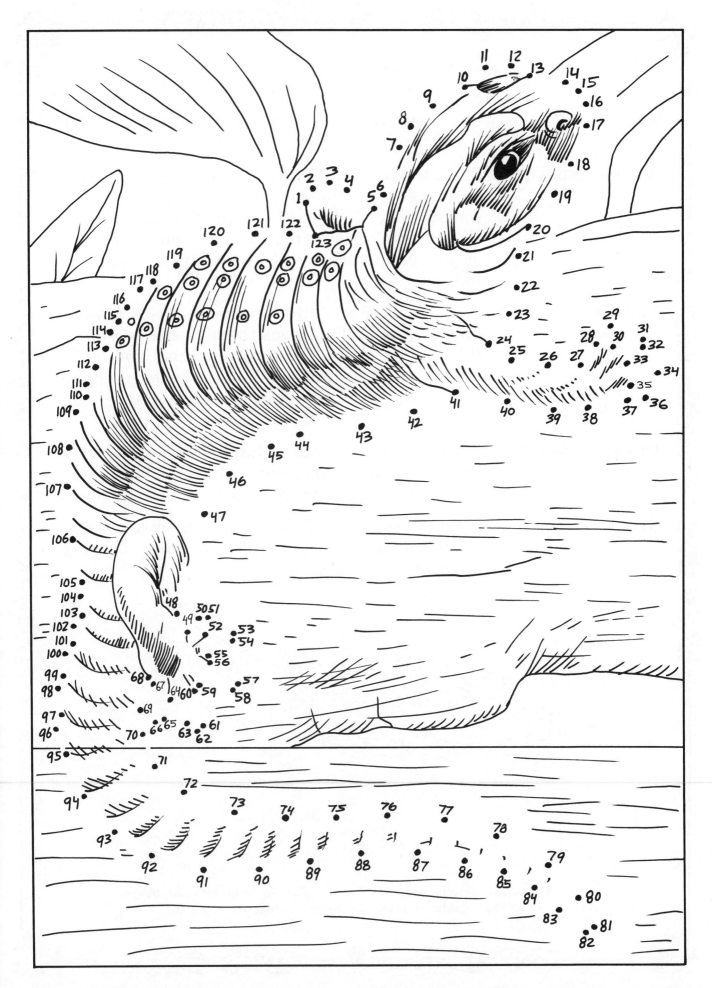

SHAMAN

WHAT IS IT?   Shamans are wise humans who have strong links with the spirit world.

WHERE AND WHEN: Since the most ancient times, they have existed in almost every culture, though they are sometimes called by other names, such as wizard, medicine man or woman, witch, sorcerer, or seer. Many people call themselves shamans today.

ABILITIES: A shaman can see into the spiritual world, where others cannot. This gives them special powers: the power to know the future, to heal and to hurt, to communicate with animals, to interpret events, and even sometimes to change the weather.

DID YOU KNOW?   A person may become a shaman because one of his parents or grandparents was one, or he or she may be called by the spirits to become one.

STORY: Sometimes a shaman is taken over by a god or spirit and does the dance of that being—singing or speaking for him or her.

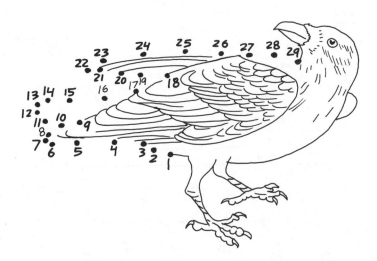

**A shaman usually uses his spirit guide to help him do magic.
That guide is often an animal, such as a raven.**

SORCERER'S STONE

WHAT IS IT?   A magical stone, also known as the philosopher's stone. Many wizards tried to make this object out of base matter.

WHERE AND WHEN: Legends of the Sorcerer's Stone were found in the first century in Egypt.

ABILITIES: The Sorcerer's Stone was thought to give eternal life and limitless wealth.

DID YOU KNOW?   Anything this stone touches turns into gold. Ground up and made into a drink, it was said to cure all disease and give eternal life.

STORY: In 1666, a stranger approached a Dutch physician known as Helvetius with three pieces of transparent crystal with a misty glow. The stranger claimed that these crystals were the philosopher's stone. Soon Helvetius was able to make the crystals change their color from bright green to blood red by cooling them. When they had completely cooled, he had pure gold.

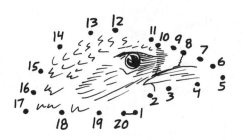

Here are two of the four mysterious stages of alchemy:
"The Head of the Crow" and "The Red Lion."

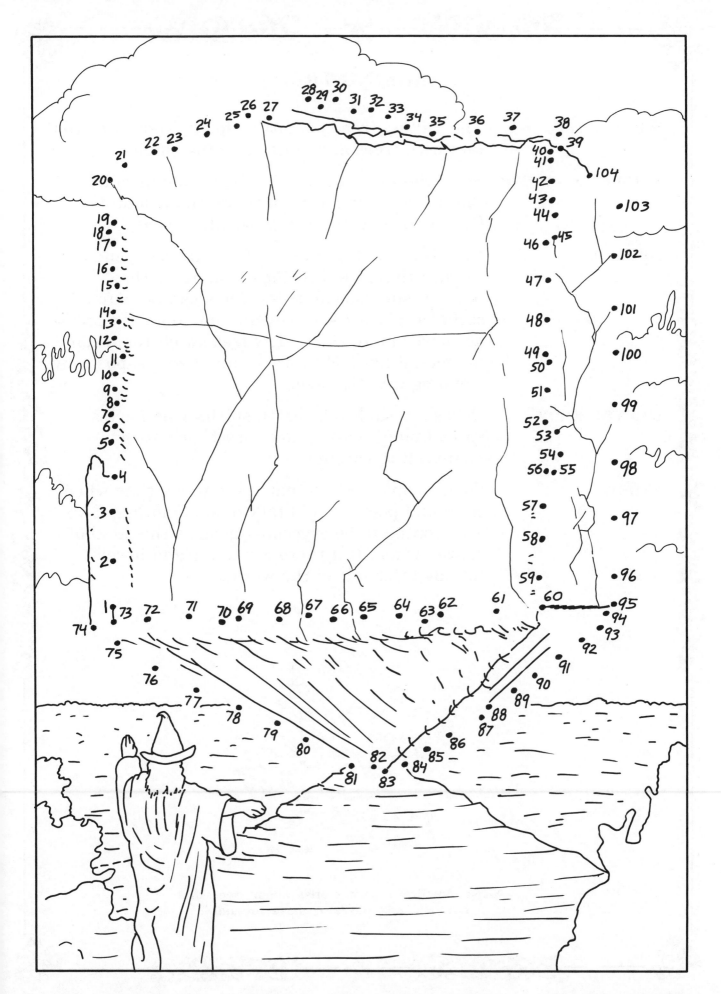

TALKING TREE

WHAT IS IT? The talking tree is a nature spirit. Many wizards talk with trees and most all living things.

WHERE AND WHEN: Since the most ancient times, people have felt that trees could speak to them. In ancient Greece, people called tree spirits dryads.

ABILITIES: Dryads are not immortal. Their lives depend on the health and well-being of the trees they inhabit, such as oak trees. They can be found in secluded places. Very shy and nonviolent, they are never more than a few feet away from their individual tree. They are thought to disappear by stepping into the tree.

DID YOU KNOW? Devas are said to be earth spirits who have a special plant, tree, whole forest, or entire mountain to care for.

STORY: Some people believe that there was a time when trees and people could talk to one another. Elves are reputed to be especially good at this kind of conversation. But there are fewer and fewer talking trees left in the world.

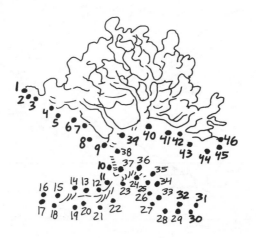

Native Americans have stories about trees that not only talk but also move around!

TEA LEAF READING

WHAT IS IT?   A wizard could use tea leaves to tell what might happen in the future. This is called tasseomancy—tasseo meaning cup and mancy meaning prophecy.

WHERE AND WHEN: This custom started in China in the sixth century.

ABILITIES: Tea leaves can tell you the shape of things to come. They could reveal things like danger, romance, disappointment, or travel.

DID YOU KNOW?   Tea didn't come to the West until 1609, and it wasn't until the middle of the 1800s that tea drinking was widespread in Europe.

STORY: Even before tea made it to the West, the ancient Romans used to tell fortunes by looking at what was left in a glass of wine after the wine was drunk. This practice is called oinomancy.

Here are some of the symbols you might see at the bottom of a cup and what they mean.

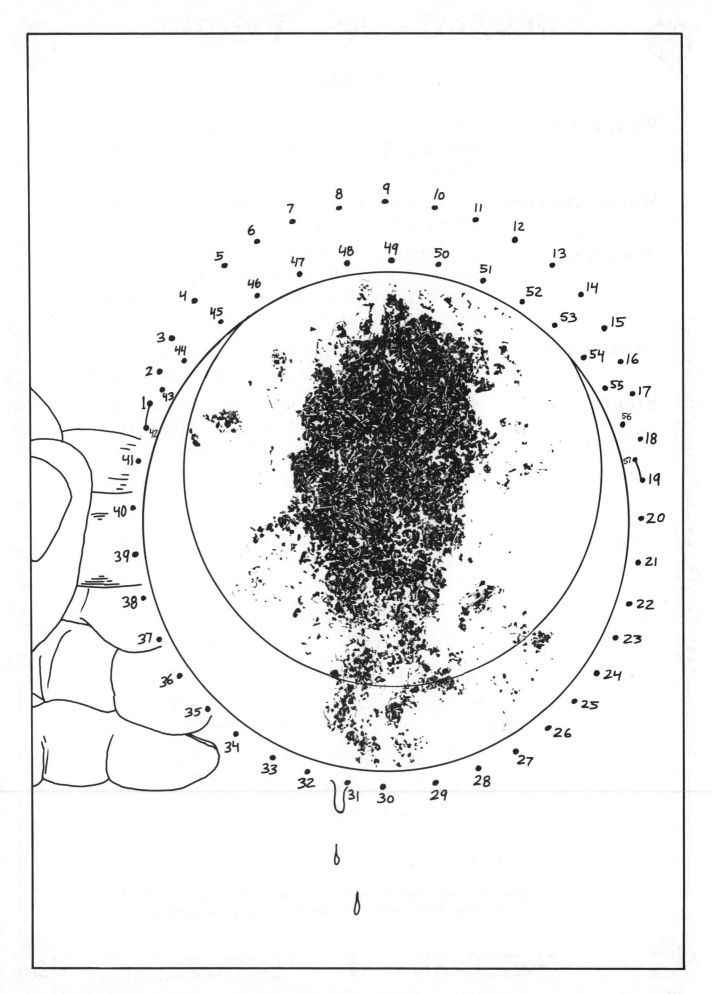

TOAD

WHAT IS IT? The toad has been associated with poison and evil since 600 B.C. Wizards use toads in their charms.

WHERE AND WHEN: Wizards and witches have long been thought to keep toads for their magical work.

ABILITIES: As a familiar, a toad could be sent out to cause mischief. It could also be used to help break in a new witch, who might be made to kiss it. The toad was also used in potions and charms.

DID YOU KNOW? At one time, witches would name their toads and could be seen dressing them up in fancy clothes.

STORY: To make themselves invisible, witches were supposed to have rubbed themselves with a lotion made from the spit of toads.

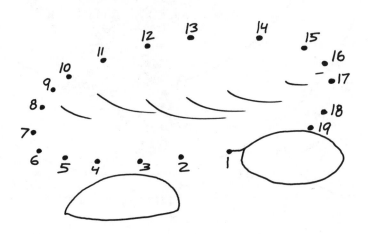

Toadstones are said to bring good luck. They are supposed to come from inside the heads of very old toads.

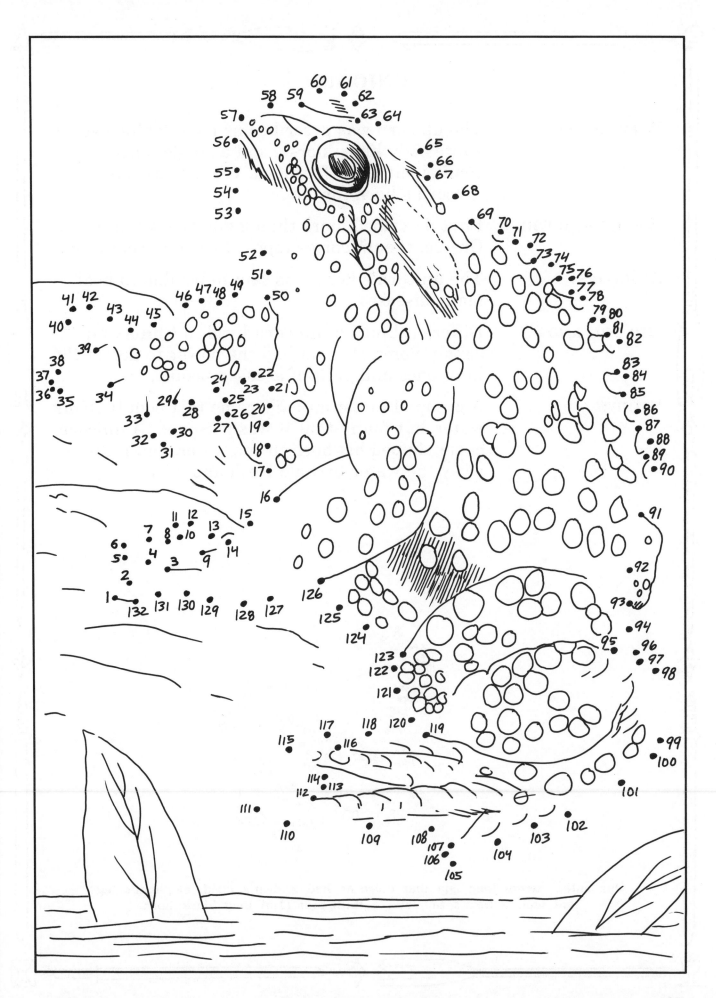

UNICORN

WHAT IS IT? The unicorn was described as having blue eyes, a white body like a horse, and a single horn coming out of its forehead. Wizards used a unicorn's horn for magic.

WHERE AND WHEN: First described more than 2,000 years ago in Greece, the unicorn supposedly came from India.

ABILITIES: The unicorn's horn was said to be able to heal many diseases.

DID YOU KNOW? Different kinds of unicorn lived in China and Japan. Some of them had the power to detect the innocence and guilt of accused people.

STORY: A group of forest animals came to a pool to drink water, but found that it was poisoned. A unicorn came, dipped his horn in the water, and right away the water became fresh and clean.

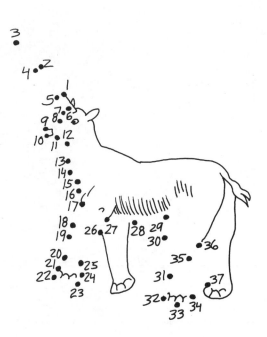

One author wrote long ago that unicorns had a deer's head, elephant's legs and feet, a boar's tail, and a three-foot (1m) long black horn.

69

WATER WIZARDRY

WHAT IS IT? Water wizardry or "dowsing" is the art of finding water or treasure by sensing the small movements or sounds made by a forked rod held in the dowser's hand.

WHERE AND WHEN: The art is ancient, going at least as far back as the 12th century, when we read of the first recorded dowser named Thomas Lethgridge. He used a pendulum.

ABILITIES: Dowsers were often used by early farmers to help decide where to place a well. A special rod might have increased power. For example, a rod made from wood obtained on Midsummer's Eve was supposed to be most effective for finding treasure.

DID YOU KNOW? Usually the rod would be forked, and if the dowser felt a pull on the left side of it, it would signify an underground stream. If the rod pulled on the right, it was more likely a stream of energy below the ground.

STORY: To use the dowsing rod, the wizard had to hold his body as straight as possible and walk forward with the rod in front of him, thinking about what he sought.

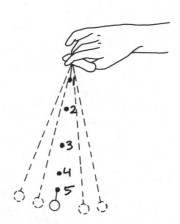

Dowsing rods are still used today. So is another wizard's tool, the pendulum, which works like a dowsing rod but can be used to answer different kinds of questions.

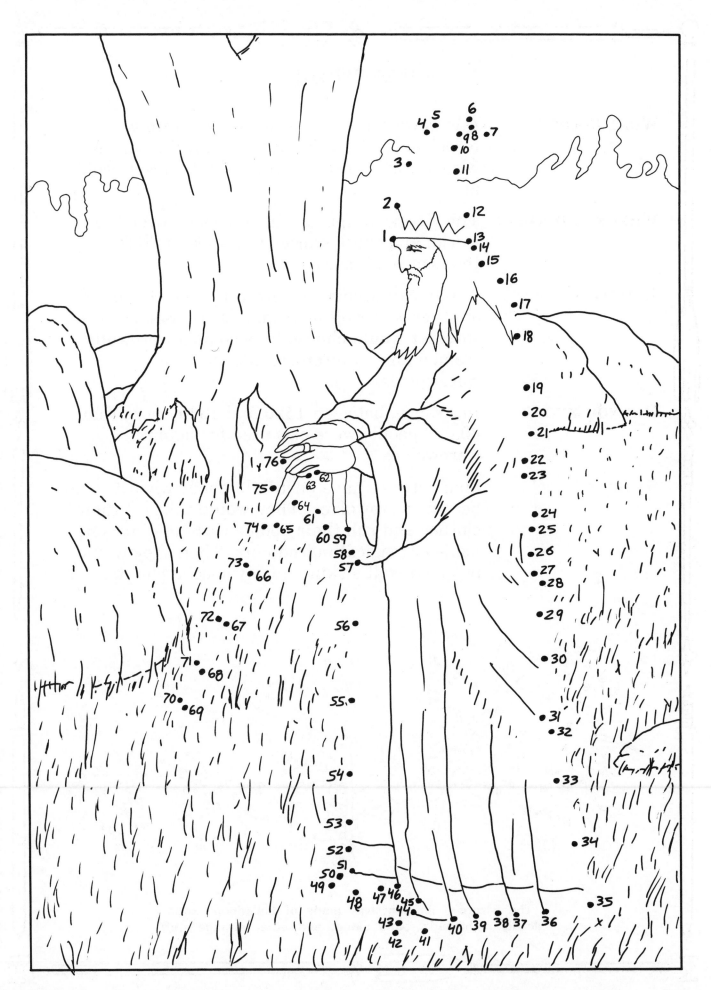

WEREWOLF

WHAT IS IT?
A werewolf is a person who turns into a ferocious wolf on the night of a full moon. A wizard can transform himself into a werewolf at will.

WHERE AND WHEN:
The werewolf appears in stories all over the world, and these stories have been told for thousands of years.

ABILITIES:
A man can become a werewolf from the bite of another werewolf or from a curse. Sometimes a sorcerer would choose to become a werewolf. Women and children can also become werewolves.

DID YOU KNOW?
In France, between 1520 and 1630, more than 30,000 people were executed for being werewolves.

STORY:
Many stories have been told about wizards who became werewolves. They would take off their clothes and rub their bodies with an ointment made of magical ingredients. Then they would put on a wolf's skin and say special chants.

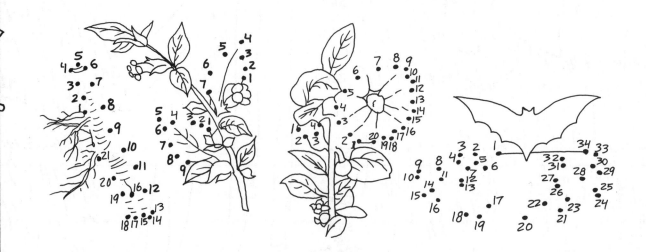

The wizard's ointment was made of belladonna root, deadly nightshade, bat's blood, and other strange stuff.

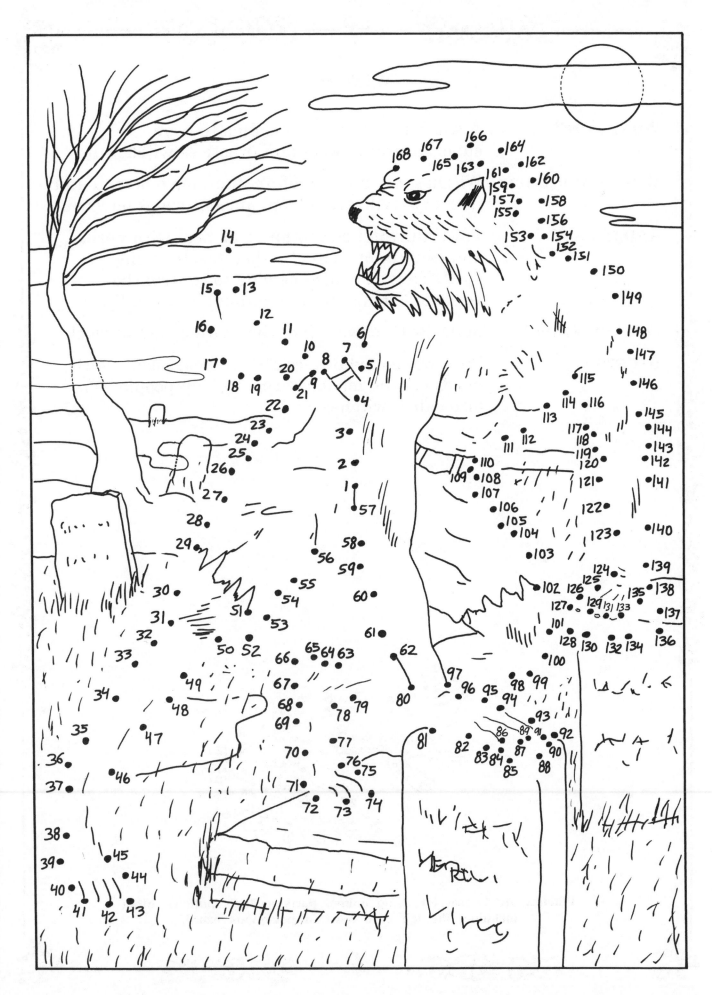

WITCH

WHAT IS IT? A witch is anyone who claims to have supernatural powers and practices witchcraft.

WHERE AND WHEN: Witches, of one kind of another, have been found in every civilization from ancient times onward.

ABILITIES: Powerful witches can harm or heal with herbs, and can kill or help at a distance by using a spell. They may also be able to control the weather, change into an animal, or even fly.

DID YOU KNOW? Males with powers like these are called warlocks.

STORY: Wise women who were able to heal people with herbs or who made charms to help people were also called witches.

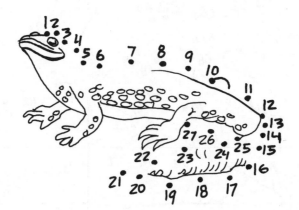

Witches are known for using animal parts in their potions, often including the tail of a newt, a poisonous lizard.

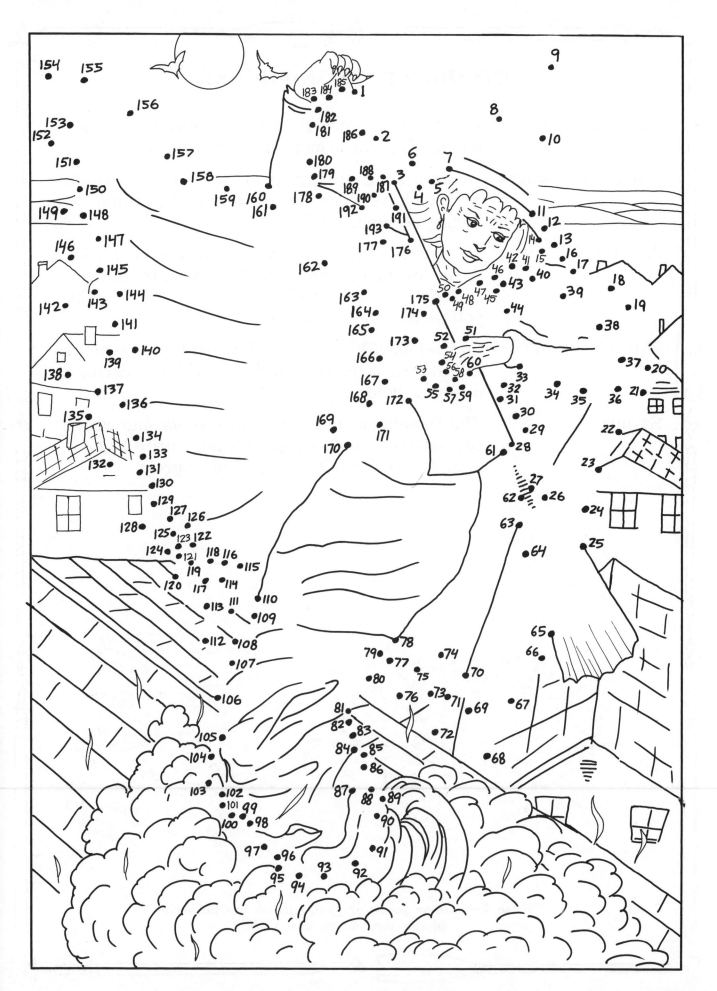

WIZARD'S HATS AND ROBES

WHAT ARE THEY?　Wizards wear special hats and robes for doing magic. The hat is usually shaped like a cone.

WHERE AND WHEN:　We know that at least as far back as the Druids, wizards have worn special hats and clothing during ceremonies.

ABILITIES:　Some hats have particular magical powers, like never falling off the head of the wizard. Some will give you good luck, make you silly, or make you unable to stop talking.

DID YOU KNOW?　Cone-shaped hoods are still worn by some monks in Catholic countries, different orders wearing different colors.

STORY:　The Druids usually wore white robes and white cone-shaped hoods covering their entire heads. Sometimes they also wore blue or green.

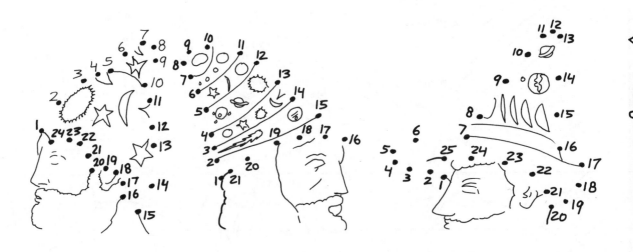

These hats, some made of gold, picture the movement of the sun, moon, and stars.

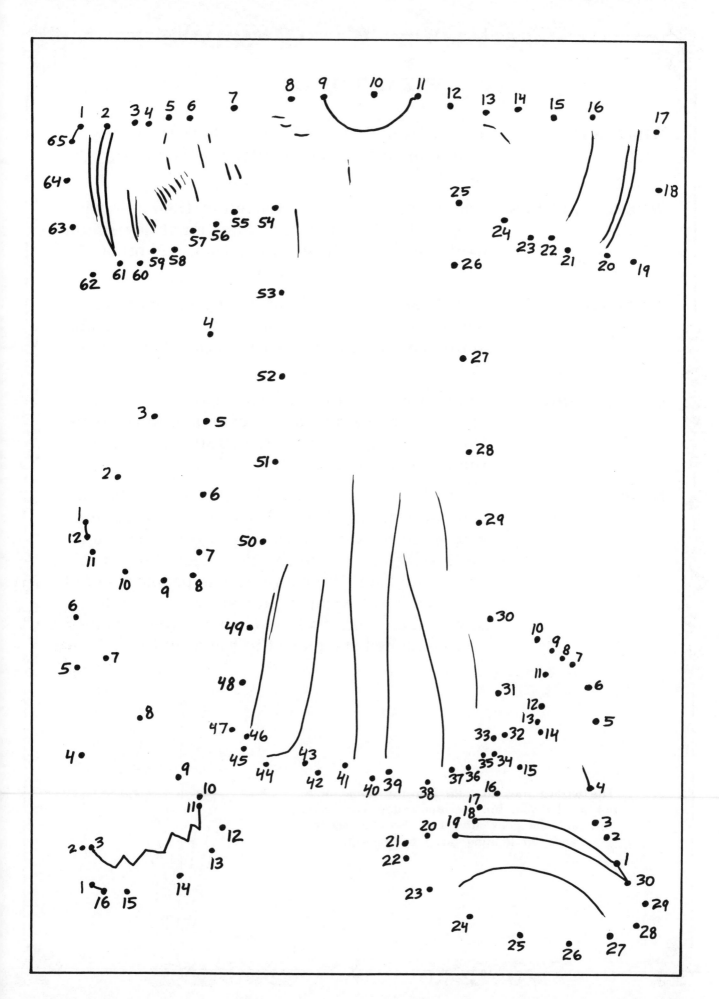

WIZARD OF OZ

WHAT IS IT? The great and powerful Wizard of Oz was a character in the books written by L. Frank Baum.

WHERE AND WHEN: The Wizard of Oz was written in 1900 and was supposed to take place in the current day. Baum wrote 14 Wizard books altogether, and other writers followed up with more.

ABILITIES: The Wizard of Oz did not have great magical powers, but he did have a lot of wisdom and an ability to see into the hearts of people and give them what they needed.

DID YOU KNOW? There are many differences between the book and the famous movie. For example, in the book Dorothy's magical slippers are silver, while in the movie they are ruby.

STORY: In the book, the wizard began as a ventriloquist who later became a balloonist for a circus. One day, when he went up the ropes got twisted and he floated high above the clouds and landed in a green and beautiful country. The people thought he was a great wizard and were willing to do anything he said. So he had them build a palace and he named the place the Emerald City.

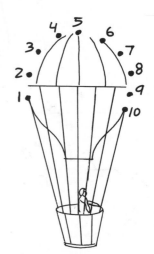

The wizard tries to take Dorothy home in a hot air balloon, but Dorothy's dog Toto runs off and she goes after him. So the wizard ends up floating away by himself.

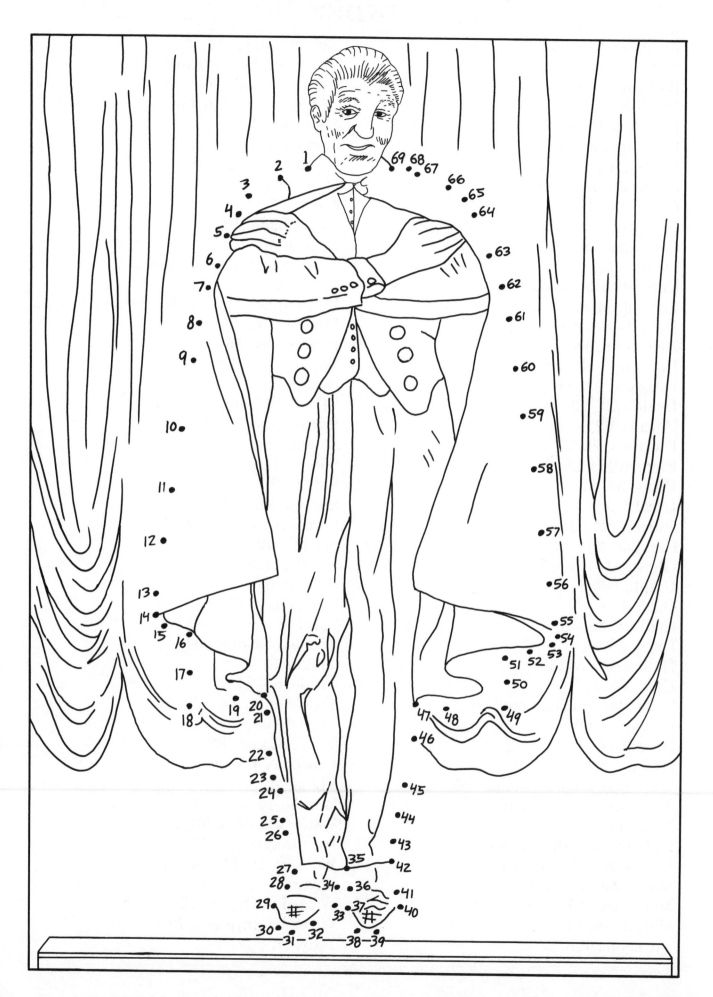

79

INDEX